NAPOLEON HILL: THE RARE TEACHINGS OF NAPOLEON HILL

Volume 1

By Patrick Doucette

***

Published by Kindle

NAPOLEON HILL: THE RARE TEACHINGS OF NAPOLEON HILL

Volume 1

Table of Contents

Introduction

To introduce this magnificent work of motivation and inspiration I would simply like to paraphrase an excerpt from the work itself:

"You can have confidence in your ability to use your mind and make that mind create the circumstances that you want created; and that's the condition and the operation of the mind of any successful person. And that's going to be the condition of your mind when you get through this information!"

This transcription has been meticulously prepared from speeches that Napoleon Hill gave to groups of students almost 100 years ago and yet the powerful and inspirational messages are as relevant today as they ever have been.

This rare reproduction will allow you to absorb the life transforming training at your own pace through the written words of Napoleon Hill as he taught them in a live personal setting with attentive students many of whom were inspired to go on and achieve great financial success; now you have the opportunity to accomplish your goals and dreams with the help of this superb instruction.

Remember that this is a direct transcription from live speeches so sometimes the grammar and tempo of the writing may seem a bit peculiar; but as you slowly absorb the words, it will start to feel as if Napoleon Hill is speaking directly to you!

This training is timeless and powerful and is a must read for anyone that wants to move forward towards success using principles that have inspired more millionaires than any other training in recorded history. Enjoy and prosper!

~ Patrick Doucette

Chapter 1 - Purpose & Plan

Now then, let's break down the lesson on Definiteness of Purpose and see exactly what it means; why it's the starting point of all achievement. Because it is the starting point of all individual achievements, and a definite purpose must be accompanied by a definite plan for its attainment followed by appropriate action.

Now you have to have a purpose, you have to have a plan and you have to have to start putting that plan into action. And ladies and gentleman it's not too important that your plan be sound. It is in fact not too important; because if you find that you've adopted a plan that's not sound that's not working, you can always change. You can modify your plan.

But it is very important that you be definite about what it is you are going after; about what your purpose is; that must be very definite. There can be no if's or and's about it and you will see before you get through this lesson why it's got to be definite. Now, just to understand this philosophy to read or to hear me talk about it wouldn't be of very much value to you. The value will come when you begin to form your own patterns from this philosophy and put it into work in your daily lives and your business and your professions or in your jobs or in your human relations. That's where the benefits will really come.

Chapter 2 - Programming the Subconscious

The second premise; all individual achievements are the result of a motive or a combination of motives. I just want to impress upon you that you have no right to ask anybody to do anything at any time without ...what?...without giving that person an adequate motive. And incidentally that' the warmth and the whoomf of all salesmanship. The ability to plant in the mind of the prospective buyer an adequate motive for his buying; learning to deal with people by planting in their minds adequate motives for their doing the things that you want them to do.

Now there are a lot of people who call themselves salesman who have never heard of the nine basic motives. Who do not know that they have no right to ask for a sale until they have planted a motive in the mind of the buyer for his buy.

The third premise. Any dominating idea plan or purpose held in the mind through repetition of thought, any dominating idea plan or purpose held in the mind through repetition of thought and emotionalized with a burning desire for it's realization is taken over by the subconscious section of the mind and acted upon through whatever natural and logical means that may be available.

Now in that paragraph you've got a tremendous lesson in psychology. If you want the mind to pick up an idea, and to form a habit, so that the mind will automatically act upon that idea; you've got to tell the mind what you want over and over and over again. No end to it.

When Mr. Coué came over here some years ago with his famous formula; "day by day in every way I'm getting better and better", he cured thousands of people but a very great number more than that he didn't cure and I wonder if you would know why? There was no desire, there was no feeling put into that statement, you might just as well blow in the wind as to make a statement unless you put some feeling back of it. Unless you believe it. And incidentally if you tell yourself anything often enough you will get to where you will believe it, even a lie. It is funny isn't it, but it happens to be true. You know there are people who tell little white lies and sometimes they're not so white at that until they get to where they get to believe them themselves.

Now the subconscious mind, doesn't know the difference between right or wrong; it doesn't know the difference between positive or negative. It doesn't know the difference between a penny or a million dollars. It doesn't know the difference between success or failure. It will accept any statement that you keep repeating to it by thoughts or by words or by any other means. And incidentally it's up to you at the beginning to lay out your definite purpose; write it out so that it can be understood, memorize it and start repeating it day in and day out until your subconscious mind picks it up and automatically acts upon it.

Now this going to take a little time; you can't expect to undo overnight what you've being doing to your subconscious mind down through the years by allowing negative thoughts to get into it. You can't expect that to happen overnight. But you will find that if you emotionalize any plan that you send over to your subconscious mind and repeat it in a state of enthusiasm and back it up with a spirit of faith; if you'll do that, the subconscious mind acts not only more quickly but it acts more definitely and it acts more positively.

And the fourth premise, any dominating desire, plan or purpose which is backed by that state of mind known as faith, is taken over by the subconscious section of the mind and acted upon immediately. That state of mind, ladies and gentlemen, is the only state of mind that will produce immediate action through the subconscious mind. And when I say faith, I don't have reference to wishing or hoping or mildly believing, I don't have reference to any of those things. I have reference to a state of mind wherein whatever it is you are going to do you can see it already in a finished act before you even begin. Now that's pretty positive isn't it.

I can truthfully tell you that not ever in my whole life have I undertaken to do anything that I didn't do it unless I got careless in my desire to do it; and backed away from it or changed my mind or my mental attitude. I have never failed to do anything that I made up my mind to do and I'll tell you that you can put yourself in a frame of mind where you can do whatever you make up your mind to do unless you weaken as you go along as so many people do.

Now let's get back to this fourth premise again. Any dominating desire, plan or purpose which is backed by that state of mind known as faith, is taken over by the subconscious section of the mind and acted upon immediately. I don't know for sure, ladies and gentlemen, but I suspect that there's a relatively small number of people in the world at any one time who understand the principle of faith. Who really understand it and know how to apply. And even if you do understand it, if you don't back it up with action and make it a part of your habit life, you might just as well not understand it because faith without deeds is dead, faith without action is dead. Faith without absolute positive belief is dead.

I don't know how you're going to get any results through believing unless you put some action back of that belief. And incidentally if you tell your mind often enough that you have faith in anything, the time will come when your subconscious mind will accept that; even if you tell your mind often enough that you have faith in yourself. Have you thought what a nice thing it would be if you had such complete faith in yourself that you wouldn't hesitate to undertake to do anything you wanted to do in life? Have you ever thought what a benefit that would be to you? You know how many people there are that sell themselves short all the way through life because they don't have a right amount of confidence let alone faith? Give a guess as to the percentage. Well it's somewhere between ninety eight and a hundred percent.

The margin who do is so small that I wouldn't begin to guess just exactly what it is. But judging by the good many thousands of people that I've come into contact with and you know without my telling you that my audiences and my classes are always above average. Judging by those people I would say that it's well over 98 percent of people who never in their whole lives develop a sufficient amount of confidence in themselves to go out and to undertake and do the things they want to do in life. They accept from life whatever life hands them.

Chapter 3 - How Nature Works

Isn't it a strange thing how nature works? She gives you a set of tools. Everything that you need to attain all that you can use or aspire to have in this world. She gives you a set of tools adequate for your every need. And she rewards you bountifully for accepting and using those tools, that's all you have to do; just accept them and use them. She penalizes you beyond compare if you don't accept them and use them. Nature hates vacuums and idleness. She wants everything to be in action. And especially does she want the human mind to be in action. The mind is not different from any other part of the body if you don't use it, if you don't rely upon it, it atrophies and withers away and finally gets to where anybody can push you around. Anybody. And oftentimes you don't have the willpower to even resist or protest when people push you around.

The fifth premise. The power of thought is the only thing over which any human being has complete unquestionable means of control; a fact so astounding that it connotes a close relationship between the mind of man and infinite intelligence.

Now there are only five known things in the whole universe, ladies and gentleman, just five and out of those five is shaped everything that is in existence. From the smallest electrons and protons of matter on up to the largest suns that float out there in the heavens. Including you and me. Just five things. There's **time** and there's **space**. There's **energy** and there's **matter**. And those four things would be no good without the fifth thing. They'd be nothing; everything would be chaos. You and I wouldn't have, never could have existed without that fifth thing; what do you think it is? **A universal intelligence**.

And it reflects itself in every blade of grass, everything that grows out of the ground, in all of the electrons and protons of matter; it reflects itself in space and in time in everything that is. There is intelligence. Intelligence operating all the time. And the person who is the most successful is the one who finds ways and means of appropriating most of this intelligence through his brain and putting it into action.

This intelligence permeates the whole universe, space, time, matter, energy; everything else. And every individual has the privilege of appropriating to his own use as much of this intelligence as he chooses. He can only appropriate it by using it. Just understanding it or believing in it is not enough. You've got to put it into specialized use in some form. And the responsibility in this course mainly is to give you a pattern, a blueprint by which you can possession of your own mind and put it into operation. All you have to do is to follow the blueprint. Don't just pick out that part of which you like best and discard the other; take it all as is.

This next premise, the subconscious section of the mind appears to be the only doorway of individual approach to infinite intelligence. Now I want you to study that language very carefully. I said it appears to be, I don't know if it is and I doubt if you do and I doubt if anyone knows definitely. A lot of people have a lot of different ideas about it, but from the best intelligence that I have been able to use, best observations that I have been able to make, thorough thousands of experiences, it is true that the subconscious section of the mind is the only doorway of individual approach to infinite intelligence and it is capable of influence by the individual through the means described in this subject and with lessons. The basis of approach is faith based upon definiteness of purpose. Now there is one sentence that gives you the whole key to that paragraph. **Faith based upon definiteness of purpose.**

Do you have any idea why it is that you don't have as much confidence in yourself as you should have? Have you ever stopped to think about that? Have you ever stopped and think about why it is when you see an opportunity coming along or what you believe to be an opportunity and you begin to question your ability to embrace it and use it? Haven't you had that happen to you many times? Doesn't it happen every day?

And if you've had a chance to be closely associated with people who are very successful, you'll know that that is one thing that they're not bothered by. If they want to do something, it never occurs to them that they can't do it. I hope that in your association with Napoleon Hill Associates, you'll come to know my distinguished business associate Mr. W. Clement Stone better, because if I ever saw a man that knows the power of his mind and is willing to rely upon that mind, Mr. Stone is that man. I don't think Mr. Stone has any worries. I don't believe he would tolerate a worry. I think it would be an insult to his intelligence if he recognized that anything was worrying him.

Why? Because he has confidence in his ability to use his mind and make that mind create the circumstances that he wants created; and that's the condition and the operation of the mind of any successful mind. And that's going to be the condition of your mind when you get through this philosophy. You're going to be able to project your mind into whatever objective you choose and you'll be never any question in your mind as to whether you can do what you want to do or not. Never a question in the world.

Chapter 4 - Broadcasting

You both have a receiving set and a broadcasting station for the vibrations of thought. A fact which explains the importance of moving with definiteness of purpose instead of drifting. Since the brain may be so thoroughly charged with the nature of one's purpose that it will begin to attract the physical or material equivalence of that purpose. Get it into your consciousness that the first radio broadcasting and receiving set was the one that exists in the brain of man. And not only does it exist in the brain of man but it exists in a great many animals. I have a couple of Pomeranian dogs and they know exactly what I'm thinking sometimes before I know! They're so smart, they can tune in on it, they know when we start off for an automobile ride and know where they are going or whether not. Don't have to say a word, not a word. Because they are in constant attunement with us.

You're mind is sending out vibrations constantly and if you're a salesman and you're going to call on a prospective buyer; the sale ought to be made before you ever come into the presence of the buyer. Have you ever thought of that?

If you're going to do anything requiring the cooperation of other people, condition your mind so that you know the other fellow is going to cooperate. Why first, because the plans you're going to offer him are so fair and honest and so beneficial to him that he can't refuse it. In other words, you have a right to his cooperation. You'll be surprised I know what a change there will be in people when you convince them sending out over this broadcasting station of yours positive thoughts instead of thoughts of fear.

Now if you want a good illustration of how this broadcasting station works; you need a thousand dollars real bad, well you go down to the bank somewhere and you've got to have that thousand by the day after tomorrow or they're going to take the car back or the furniture or something else. You just have to have that thousand dollars. Why the banker can tell the moment you walk inside that door you just have to have it and he doesn't want you to have it. Isn't that funny? No it's not funny, it's tragic.

You carry the matches around in your own pocket sometimes that set your own house afire. You broadcast your thoughts and they precede you and when you get there, you find that instead of getting the cooperation you went after the other person reflects back to you what?

That state of doubt, that state of mind that you sent out ahead of you.

I used to teach salesmanship, I made my living that way for a long time while I was doing the research on this philosophy and I have taught over 30,000 salesmen, many of them now are life members of the coveted million dollar round table in the life insurance field. And if there's one thing in this world that has to be sold it's life insurance, nobody ever buys life insurance; it has to be sold.

And the first thing that I taught those people under my direction was that they must make the sale in themselves before they try to make it in the other fella. And if they don't do that they're not going to make a sale, somebody might buy something from them but they'll never make a sale unless they first make it to themselves.

Every brain a broadcasting station and a receiving set and you can attune that brain so that it'll attract only the positive vibrations released by other people. Now that's the point I am coming to and I wanted you to get. By habit you can train your own mind to pick up out of that myriad of vibrations that are floating out there constantly, train your mind to pick up only the things that are related to what you want most in life; and how do you do that?

Why you do that by keeping your mind on what you want most in life, your definite major purpose. So by repetition, by thought, by action, until finally the brain will not pick up anything not related to that definiteness of purpose. Now is that a marvelous thought? You can educate your brain so that it will absolutely refuse to pick any vibrations except those related to what you want. And ladies and gentleman, when you get your brain under control like that you will be on the path, really and truly on the beam.

Chapter 5 - Benefits of Definiteness of Purpose

Now let's see what are some of the benefits of definiteness of purpose. First of all definiteness of purpose automatically develops self reliance: personal initiative, imagination, enthusiasm, self discipline and concentration of effort. All of these being pre-requisites for success of vital importance. Now that's quite an array of things that you really developed. You developed through definiteness of purpose, that is to say knowing what you want, having a plan for getting it, having your mind occupied mostly with the carrying out of that plan. And if you happen to adopt a plan and unless you are an unusual person, you're almost sure to adopt some plans that are not going to work so well. When you find out that your plan is not right, immediately discard it and get another one. And keep on until you find one that will work.

And in the process of doing this; just remember one thing that maybe somewhere along the line that infinite intelligence being gifted with a great deal of wisdom might have a plan for you better than the one you had yourself. Have an open mind. If you adopt a plan that can't carry out your major purpose or minor purpose and it doesn't work well, dismiss that plan and ask for guidance from infinite intelligence. And you may get that guidance, what can you do to be sure that you will get it? A while you can believe is you'll get it, you can believe that you'll get it. And it's not gonna hurt if you say out loud orally that you believe it.

I suspect that the creator can know your thoughts but I found if you express yourself with a lot of enthusiasm it doesn't hurt any. And I'm sure that it doesn't hurt in arousing your subconscious mind. When I wrote 'Think and Grow Rich', the original title of it was '13 Steps to Riches' and both the publisher and I knew that that was not a box office title, we had to have a million dollar title. Well they went ahead and set the book up in type and the publisher kept prodding me very day to give him the title that I wanted and I wrote five or six hundred titles and there weren't any of them that were any good, not any of them.

And then one day he scared the dickens out of me, he called me and said well he said "Tomorrow morning I've to have that title and if you don't have one I have one that's a humdinger".

And I said "what is it?" He said, "we're going to call it Use Your Noodle and get the Boodle."

I said, "My goodness you'll ruin me". "Why is that, this is a dignified book. And that's a flippant title, why that would ruin the book and me too".

Well he said. "whether it will or not, that's the title unless you give me a better one by tomorrow morning."

Now I want you to follow this incident because it's potent with food for thought. What I'm now telling you. I went in that night and sat down on my bed as I was going to, on the side of the bed and I had a talk with my subconscious mind. And I said, "Now look here ol' sub, you and I have gone a long way together and you've done a lot of things for me and some things to me thanks to my ignorance. But I've got to have a million dollar title and I've got to have it tonight, do you understand that?" I got to talking so loudly that the man in the partment above me thumped on the floor. And I don't blame him, I guess he thought I was quarreling with my wife or something.

Well I really gave the subconscious mind no doubt as to what I wanted. Now I didn't tell him, I didn't tell the subconscious mind exactly what kind of a title, I said "It's got to be a million dollar title!" I went to bed, when I, when I had charged my subconscious mind until I reached that psychological moment where I knew it was going to produce what I wanted. And if I hadn't, if I hadn't of gotten to that point, I would be up there still sitting up there at the side of that bed talking to my subconscious.

There is a psychological moment and you can feel it when the power of faith takes over whatever you're trying to do and says "alright you can relax, this is it".

I went to bed and about two o'clock in the morning I woke up as if somebody had shaken me real hard and as I came out of my sleep, Think and Grow Rich was in my mind. Oh boy I let out a whoop! I jumped to my typewriter, I wrote it down and I grabbed a telephone and called the publisher.

He said "what's the matter, is the town on fire or something?"; it was about 2:30 in the morning by this time.

I said "yes, you bet it is with a million dollar title".

He said, "let's have her."

I said "Think and grow Rich."

He said, "Boy you've got it!"

Yeah, I'll say we've got it. That book has grossed outside of the United States over twenty three million dollars already and probably will gross over a hundred million dollars before I pass on. And there's no end to it. A million dollars?; a multi-million dollar title. Well after the thrashing I gave my subconscious I'm not surprised that it really came over and did a good job.

Now why didn't I use that method in the first place? Isn't that a funny thing? I know the law. Why did fool around about it and temporize, why didn't I go to the source and get my subconscious mind all heated up instead of sitting down at my typewriter and writing out five or six hundred titles; why didn't I? Well I'll tell you why, for the same reason that you oftentimes know what to do but won't do it. There's no explaining the indifference of mankind towards himself. Even after you know what the law is. You'll know what the score is and you fool around until the last limit before you do anything about it.

Chapter 6 - Prayer

Just like in prayer; fool around about prayer until the time of need comes and then you're scared to death and of course you don't get any results from prayer. If you want to have results from prayer, you condition your mind so that your life is a prayer, day in and day out, every minute of your life. A constant prayer. Because it's based upon belief. Belief in your dignity and your right to tune in on infinite intelligence to have the things that you need in this world. And so it is with this human mind, you've got to condition the mind as you go along from day to day so that when any emergency arises you will be right there ready to deal with it.

Also the definiteness of purpose induces one to budget one's time and to plan day to day endeavors which lead to the attainment of one's major purpose. If you would sit down and put an hour by hour account of the actual work that you put in for each day for one week and then an hour by hour account of the time that you waste that you could devote to anything you want to if you wanted to badly enough. You're gonna get one of the shocks of your life.

We're not efficient. You have about eight hours to sleep, eight to earn a living and about eight hours of free time that you can do anything you want to with here in this country where we live. And then definiteness of purpose makes one more alert in recognizing opportunities related to the object of one's major purpose. And it inspires the courage to embrace and act upon those opportunities.

Chapter 7 - Attack!

Now we all see opportunities almost every day of our lives; which if we embrace them and acted upon them could benefit us. But there's something in us that we call procrastination. We just don't have the will, the alertness, the determination to embrace opportunities when they come along. But if you condition your mind with this philosophy, you'll not only embrace opportunities but you'll do something better; what could you do better than embrace an opportunity? **Make the opportunity!**

That's the idea. One of Napoleon's generals, the other Napoleon; came to him one day and they were fixing to attack the next morning. And this general says "Sir, the conditions, the circumstances are not just right for the attack tomorrow."

And Napoleon says, "Circumstances not right? Hell I make circumstances! Attack!"

And I have never seen a successful man yet in any business that didn't say when somebody says it can't be done, he says **"Attack!"** Attack, start where you are.

And when you get around to that curve in the road, you'll know you can't see by it until you get there, you'll always find that the road goes on around. Attack! Don't procrastinate, don't stand still, attack!

And definiteness of purpose inspires confidence in one's integrity and character. It attracts the favorable attention in other people. Have you ever thought about that? I think the whole world loves to see a person walking with his chest sticking out, walking with an atmosphere that tells the whole doggone world that he knows what he's doing and he's right on the way doing it.

Well you know, people will get out the way on the sidewalk and let you go by if you are determined to get by; and you don't have to whistle at them either or holler at them or anything of that kind. You just have to send your thoughts ahead with determination that you're going through that crowd. And believe me, they stand aside and let you go through. And the world's like that. The person who knows where they are going and is determined to get there will always find willing helpers to cooperate with them.

Now there's another very important thing, the greatest of all its benefits, that is, definiteness of purpose, it opens the way for the full exercise of that state of mind known as faith. By making the mind positive and freeing the mind from the limitations of fear and doubt and discouragement and indecision and procrastination.

The very minute that you decide upon something, you know that's what you want, you know you're going to do it. All of these negatives, that have been bothering you, they pick up their baggage and get out. They just move out. They can't live in a positive mind. Can you imagine a negative frame of mind and a positive frame of mind occupying the same space at the same time, can you imagine that? No, you can't because it can't be done. And did you know that the slightest bit of a negative mental attitude is sufficient to destroy the power of prayer? Did you know that the slightest bit of a negative mental attitude is sufficient to destroy your plan, whatever it is you are doing? Carrying out your definiteness of purpose.

You have to move with courage, with faith, with determination in connection with carrying out your definite major purpose. And next, definiteness of purpose makes one success conscious. You know what I mean by success conscious? If I said it makes one also health conscious, would you know what I meant by that? What do I mean? Why your thoughts are predominantly about health and with reference to success consciousness, your thoughts are predominantly about success. The 'can do' part of life and not the 'no-can-do'.

Did you know that the 98% of the people that can never get anywhere in life, that we talked about a while ago are 'no-can-do' people? Any circumstance that you place before them or that is placed before them or that overtakes them; immediately they fasten their attention on the 'no-can-do' part the negative part.

I'll never forget as long as I live what happened to me when Mr. Carnegie surprised me and gave me a chance to organize this philosophy. I tried in every way in the world to give him the reasons I could think of; and I had about six; six reasons why I couldn't do it.

I didn't have sufficient education, I didn't have the money, I didn't have the influence, I didn't know what the word philosophy meant, well, there was about two others that immediately popped into my mind and I was trying to get my mouth open to tell Mr. Carnegie that I thanked him for the compliment that he paid me but what is going on in my mind was I was doubting that Mr. Carnegie was such a good judge of human nature as he had been reported to be when he was picking me to do a job like that. Now that's what went on in my mind.

But there were silent persons standing looking over my shoulder and he said go ahead and tell him you can do it, spit it out. I said "Yes Mr. Carnegie I will accept the commission and you can depend upon it that I will complete it!" He reached over and grabbed by the hand and he said, 'I not only like what you said but I like the way you said it." That's what I was waiting for. He saw that my mind was on fire with belief that I could do it even though I hadn't the slightest asset to give me a beginning other than my determination that I would get the assets necessary to create this philosophy.

And if I had wavered in the slightest, if I had of said to Mr. Carnegie, "Well yes, Mr. Carnegie, I'll do my best," I am sure, I never asked him about this, but I am sure that he would have taken the opportunity away from me instantly. It would have indicated that I wasn't too determined to do it.

"Yes, Mr. Carnegie, you can depend upon me sir to complete it!" And you're living witnesses here, although Mr. Carnegie is long since been gone, you're living witnesses that Mr. Carnegie didn't pick wrongly.

He knew what he was about, he had found something in the human mind, in my mind that he had been searching for for years. He found it, I didn't know it's value but I found out the value of it later and I want you to recognize the value of it because you have that same thing in your mind. That same capacity to know what you want and to be determined to get it even though you don't know where to make the first start.

And what does make a great man? Give me a definition, what makes a great man or a great woman? Do you have any idea what greatness is? Greatness is the ability to recognize the power of your own mind to embrace it and use it. That's what makes greatness. And in my book of rules, every man and every woman can become truly great by the simple process of recognizing his or her own mind, embracing it and using it.

Chapter 8 - Detailed Instructions for Definite Major Purpose

Now your instructions for applying the principle of definite major purpose, and these instructions are to be carried out to the letter. Don't overlook any part of it. First write out a clear statement of your major purpose. Sign it. Commit it to memory and repeat it overly at least once a day in the form of a prayer or of an affirmation if you choose. You can see the advantage of this because it places your faith in your creator squarely back of you.

Now I've found from experience, ladies and gentlemen, here is the weakest spot in the students' activities. They read this and they say, "Well that's simple enough, what's the use of going to the trouble of writing it out. You might just as well not have this lesson if you're going to take that attitude to it. You must write it out, you must go through the physical act of translating a though into, onto paper and then you must memorize it and then you must start talking to your subconscious mind about it. Give that subconscious mind a pretty good idea of what it is you want.

And it won't hurt any if you remember the story I told you in the first half of the lesson tonight about what I did to get my million dollar book title. It won't do a bit of harm if you give your subconscious mind to understand from here on out that you're the boss and that you're gonna do something about it.

But you can't expect the subconscious mind nor anything else to help you if you don't know what it is you want; if you're not definite about it. Ninety-eight out of every hundred people, taking a cross section of humanity in general do not know what they want in life and consequently never get it. They take whatever life hands them.

Now in addition to your definite major purpose, you can have minor purposes, as many as you want, provided they lead you in the direction of your major purpose. Provided they are related to or lead you in the direction of your major purpose. Your whole life should be devoted to carrying out your major purpose in life. Find out what it is you want and incidentally it's all right to be modest like I am, (chuckle), when you go asking for what you want; but don't be too modest.

Reach out and ask for a bounty. Ask for the things you are sure you're entitled to but in asking be sure that you don't overlook the subsequent instructions I am going to give you; about what it is you are going to give in return for what it is you expect.

Second, right out a clear definite outline of the plan or plans by which you intend to achieve the object of your purpose and state the time in which you intend to attain it. And describe it in detail precisely what you intend to give in return for the realization of the object of your purpose.

Make you plans flexible enough to permit changes any time you're inspired to do so. Remembering that infinite intelligence may present you with a better plan than yours and oftentimes will if you are definite about what you want.

Have any of you every had a hunch that you couldn't ascribe, that you couldn't explain away? You know what a hunch is? It's your subconscious mind trying to get an idea over to you and oftentimes you are too indifferent to even let the subconscious mind talk to you for a few moments. I've heard people say, "Well I've had the darnedest fool idea today." But that darned fool idea, you know, might have been a million dollar idea if you'd have listened to it and done something about it.

Have great respect for these hunches that come because there is something outside of yourself trying to communicate with you undoubtedly.

I have a great respect for these hunches that come to me and they come to me constantly and I find them always related to something that my mind has been dwelling upon, something that I want to do; something that I'm engaged in.

Write out a clear definite outline of the plan or plans and state the maximum of time within which you intend to attain it. Now that timing is important, very important. Don't write out your definite major aim if I intend to become the best salesman in the world in or that I intend to become the best employee in my organization or that I intend to make a lot of money; that's not definite.

Whatever it is that you consider to be your major objective in life, write it out clearly and time it.

I intend to attain within blank number of years, so and so, and then go ahead and describe so and so, what it is. And then in the next paragraph down below, I intend to give in return for the thing that I request so and so and then go ahead and describe it.

Now this business of timing, you know nature has a system of timing in everything. If you're a farmer, you go out and plant some wheat in a field, you go out and you prepare that ground, you sow the wheat at the right season of the year. And then after you sow it, you go back the next day with a harvester and start harvesting, the very next day. Well isn't anybody gonna catch me up on that one?

What do you wait for? For nature to do her part! Infinite intelligence or God or whatever you want it's not a matter of what you call it, we're talking about the same thing but there's an intelligence that does its' part if you do your part first.

Intelligence is not going to direct you to nor attract to you the object of your major purpose unless you know what it is and unless you properly time it. It'd be quite ridiculous if you started out with only a mediocre talent and said you were going to make a million dollars within the next thirty days; it be quite ridiculous. In other words make your major purpose within reason of what you know you are able to deserve.

Next, keep your major purpose strictly to yourself, except in so far as you will receive further instructions on this subject in the lesson on the master mind. Now why do I suggest that you keep your major purpose to yourself? Well, the reason of course that you don't disclose your major purpose to other people is that there are a lot of idle curious people in this world who like to stand on the sidelines and stick their toes out when you go by especially if you've got a high head and look like you're going to accomplish more in life than they are.

And for no good reason at all, as you go along, they stick their toes out just to see you fall. They'll throw monkey wrenches in your machinery. If they don't have monkey wrenches, they'll put sand in your gearbox. But they will slow you down. Why? Because of the envy of mankind.

Now the only way to speak about your definite major purpose is in action after the fact and not before the fact, after you've achieved it. That is speak for itself. Let it speak for itself. The only way anybody can afford to boast or brag about himself is not by words but by deeds. And then if the deeds are engaged in, you don't need any words, they speak for themselves.

Now about making your plan flexible, don't become determined that the plan you worked out is perfect just because you worked it out. You'll make a mistake if you do that. Leave your plan flexible. Give it a good trial and if it's not working properly, change it.

Chapter 9 - Programming the Conscious and Subconscious

Next call your major purpose into your consciousness as often as may be practical. Eat with it. Sleep with it. And take it with you wherever you go keeping in mind the fact that your subconscious mind can thus be influenced to work for its' attainment while you sleep.

Your conscious mind is a very jealous mind, it stands guard and doesn't want anything to get by except the things that you are afraid of and the things you are very enthusiastic about; and especially the things that you are afraid of. It does let fibs sometimes get by too. But generally speaking, if you want to plant an idea in your subconscious mind, you have to do it with a tremendous amount of faith, tremendous amount of enthusiasm. You've got to rush the conscious mind so that it lets you go through to the subconscious; because of your enthusiasm and your faith.

And then repetition is a marvelous thing too. The conscious mind finally gets tired of hearing you say a thing over and over and over and says "alright, if you're bound to repeat that I can't stand here and watch you forever go on in there and take in to sub and see what he'll do with it". That's the way it works.

This conscious mind is a very contrary thing and you know it learns all of the things that won't work. Did you know that, it has a tremendous stock of things that won't work and things that are not right. It has a tremendous stock of old pieces of string, horseshoes and nails; like some misers gather up. A whole stock of those things lying around; useless trash that it's gathered. Impedimenta that you don't need and that's the kind of stuff it's feeding to your subconscious mind.

Every night just before you go to bed, you should give your subconscious mind some sort of an order for the night, what it is you want done. I should say the healing of your body, certainly the body needs repairing every day. When you lay the carcass down for sleep, then turn it over to the infinite intelligence and request your subconscious mind to go to work and heal every cell in your body; every organ, and to give you tomorrow morning a perfectly conditioned body in which the mind may function.

Don't go to bed without orders to your subconscious mind. Tell it what you want. Get in the habit of telling it what you want. You keep on long enough, it will believe you and deliver what you ask for. And therefore you better be careful about what you ask for because if you keep on asking for it, you're gonna get it.

I wonder if you wouldn't be surprised if you knew right now what you've been asking for down through the years. You ever thought of that? You've been asking for it. Sure you have. Everything that you have that you don't want, you've been asking for it. Maybe by neglect. Maybe by neglect maybe you didn't tell the subconscious mind what you really wanted and it stocked up on a lot of stuff you didn't want. It works that way.

Chapter 10 - The Greatest Purpose and The Greatest Sin

Now here's some important factors in connection with your definite major purpose. First of all, it should represent your greatest purpose in life. The one single purpose which above all others you desire to achieve and the fruits of which you are willing to leave behind you as a monument to yourself.

Now that's what your definite major purpose should be. I'm not talking about your minor purposes now, I'm talking about your major, overall purpose, your life long purpose. And believe me friends if you don't have an overall life long purpose, you're wasting, you're just wasting the better portion of your life.

The wear and tear of living is not worth the price you pay for it unless you really are aiming for something, unless you're going somewhere in life. Unless you're doing something with this opportunity here on this plane.

I imagine you're sent over here to do something. I imagine you were sent over here with a mind capable of hewing out, attaining your own destiny. And if you don't attain that, if you don't use that mind, I imagine that your life to a large extent will have been wasted; from the viewpoint of the one who sent you over.

Take possession of your mind, aim high. Don't believe because in the past, you may not have achieved much, you can't achieve in the future. Don't measure your future by your past. If you do, you're sunk. A new day is coming, you're gonna be born again. You're setting up a new pattern. You're in a new world, you're a new person. And if not why not?

I intend that every one of you shall be born again. Mentally, physically and maybe spiritually. A new aim, a new purpose; a new realization of your own individual power. And a new realization of your own dignity as a unit of mankind.

If you ask me what I believe to the greatest sin of mankind, I bet you'd be surprised as what my answer would be. What would yours be. What do think the greatest sin of mankind is? The greatest sin of mankind is **neglect to use his greatest asset,** that's the greatest sin of mankind. It's bound to be that because if you use that greatest asset, you'll have everything you want and you'll have it in abundance.

You notice I didn't say you'd have everything within reason, I said you'd have everything you want and have it in abundance. I didn't put any qualifying words in there.

You're the only who can put qualifying words in there as to what you want. You're the only one that can set up limitations for yourself. Nobody else can do it for you; unless you let them.

Your major purpose or some portion of it should remain a few jumps ahead of you at all times as something to which you may look forward to with hope and anticipation. Now if you ever catch up with your major purpose and attain it, then what? What are you going to do there? Get another one, of course.

And you will have learned, by having obtained your first one, that you can attain a major purpose and the chances are when you select your next one you'll make it a bigger objective than you did your first one. If your objective is to acquire material riches why don't aim too high for the first year. Work a twelve month plan within reason and watch how easy you can attain it and then next year double it. Then next year double that.

One's major purpose should keep a few jumps ahead of them. What's the purpose of that? Why not lay out a definite purpose that you can catch up with, well just tomorrow, say? Well now obviously if you do that, your definite major purpose is not gonna be very extensive is it? And you're not gonna have the fun of pursuit. You know the fun of pursuit is a great thing.

If you found success, if you found your objective, why then there's no fun in it but you have to turn around and start after something else. Life is less interesting when one has no definite purpose to be obtained other than that of merely living. The hope of future achievement in connection with a major purpose is among the greatest of man's pleasures.

Sorry is the man indeed who's caught up with himself and no longer has anything to do. I've found a lot of them; they're all miserable.

No you've got to keep active. Keep doing something. Keep working. Keep an objective ahead of you. One's major purpose may, and it generally does, consist of that which can be obtained only by a series of day to day and month to month and year to year steps. Because it is something which should be so designed as to consume an entire lifetime of endeavor.

It should harmonize with one's occupation, business or profession. For each days' work should enable one to come one day nearer to the attainment of his major purpose in life.

I feel sorry, indeed I feel sorry for the individual who is just working day in and day out in order to have something to eat and some clothes to wear and a place to sleep. I feel sorry for that kind of a person who has no aim beyond other than to just enough to exist on.

I can't imagine anybody in this class satisfied sitting down with an existence. I think you want to live. I think you want abundance. I think you want everything that's necessary for you to do the thing you want to do in life; including money.

Chapter 11 - Relationships

One's major purpose may, and generally does, consist of that which can be attained only by a series of day to day or month to month steps. Now remember that when you start in pursuit of your definite major purpose. One's major purpose may consist of many different combinations of lesser aims; such as the nature of one's occupation which should be something of their own choice. When you come to write out your definite major purpose, you write it out like planks in a platform. Number one, so and so; number two so and so, and somewhere along there, right near the head be sure that you include in your definite major purpose perfect harmony between yourself and your mate.

Think that's important? Do you know of anything more important than that? Do you know of anything, any human relationship more important than that of a man and his wife? No of course you don't, I'll answer that one for you. Nobody does. And have you ever heard of a relationship between a man and wife where there was not harmony? Have you ever seen a thing like that? You have huh? Yeah,; I'll answer that for you too; I know you have. It's not pleasant is it? It's not pleasant to even be around people who are not in step with one another.

Well you can be harmonious and there is where you ought to start applying your master mind relationship first. Your wife or your husband should be your first mastermind ally. Maybe you'll have to go back and court him or her over again but alright that's nice too. I don't know if I ever did anything in my life that I enjoyed as much as courting. A wonderful experience. Go back and court the gal over again; or the man. A wonderful experience.

Or if you're not on the right kind of terms with your business associate or your fellow worker or the people you work with every day. Go back and rededicate yourself to the business of striking off on a new basis. You'll be surprised what a little confession on your part will do. A wonderful thing; confession is really a marvelous thing.

Most people claim they have too much pride to confess their weaknesses. I tell you it's a good thing to get that out, get some of your weaknesses out of your system by confession. Acknowledge that maybe you're not perfect, well nigh perfect but not entirely perfect. Maybe the other fell will say "well, come to think of it neither am I". And then your off to the races.

Rededicate yourself to a better relationship with the people you come into contact every day. Whoever they may be. What a wonderful thing it is, you can do that , you can handle it, I know you can. You know most of these inharmonies in human relations is due to the neglect of people. You just neglect your human relations. You can do it if you wanted to do it.

And the budgeting of income and expenses so as to provide for the accumulation of a definite amount for old age and security. The security of loved ones and so forth. And the budgeting of time so as to provide whatever income that is necessary to support ones plan for the attainment of a definite major purpose; that should be a part of your definite major purpose.

Write out your platform of life and include down under these minor purposes the things that are related to your major purpose. The things that you're going to have to get in step by step movement up toward your major purpose.

And a definite plan for developing harmony in all of your relations especially these: in the home, where one works, where one plays or relaxes. The human relationship plank is the most important one in connection with one's major aim since the aim is attainable very largely through the cooperation of others.

Have you ever thought of that; that the things that you do in life that they're worthwhile have to be done through harmonious cooperation with other people. And how are you going to get that harmonious cooperation if you don't cultivate people? If you don't understand them; if you don't make allowances for their weaknesses?

Did you ever have a friend that appreciated your trying to reform him or change his mind about something? Do you like to have a friend come around and try to reform you? No you don't, nobody does. But there are certain things you can do for a friend by example that's a might effective way of doing it.

But start in to tell a man where he's wrong and chance are that he'll have business around the corner. The next time he sees you coming, he'll get on the other side of the street.

In your human relations, you can develop a marvelous relationship but you can't do it by criticizing people, by harping upon their faults, because we all have faults. A better thing to do is to talk about a person' virtues and his good qualities. I have never seen a person yet so lowly that he didn't have some good qualities. And if you'll concentrate on those good qualities that person on whom you're concentrating will go out his way and lean over backwards to make sure that you're not disappointed.

One should not hesitate to choose a major aim which may be for the time being out of his reach; for one may always prepare himself to attain pretty much any desired purpose in life. Certainly when I chose as my definite major purpose the organizing and taking to the world of the first practical philosophy of the individual achievement it was way beyond my reach.

And what do you think it was that kept me down to twenty years of unproductive effort of research; what do you think it was that kept me striving and struggling in face of the fact that the majority of the people that I knew were criticizing me? What do you think it was? I had to have an abundance of faith and I had to keep that faith alive by moving, moving always as if I knew in advance that I was going to complete the task that Mr. Carnegie assigned to me.

There were times when it looked as if what my friends and relatives were saying about me was absolutely true, and in a sense it was. That I was wasting my time. From their viewpoint and their measuring sticks and their standards I was wasting twenty years of my time. But from the viewpoint of the millions of people that have benefited and will benefit by my work during those twenty years, I was not wasting my time.

You can't fail!... Unless you think you can. If you think you can fail, then you can. If you stay around me long enough I'll get you so you're not going to think you're gonna fail. You'll know you're not going to fail.

Chapter 12 - Examples From Nature

Our greatest demonstration of the universal application of the principle of definiteness of purpose can be seen by observing how nature applies it as follows. And there's a great string of applications the way nature moves with definiteness of purpose and ladies and gentleman, if there is anything in this universe that's definite, it's the laws of nature. They don't deviate, they don't temporize, they don't subside. You can't go around them, you can't avoid them, and however you can learn their nature and adjust yourself to them and benefit by them; nobody ever heard of the law of gravity being suspended not even for one fraction of a second; it never has been done and never will be. Because nature's whole setup throughout the whole universe, systems of universe perhaps, is so definite that everything moves with precision like clockwork.

If you want an example of the necessity of an individuals' moving with definiteness, you only have to have a smattering of understanding of the sciences to see the way that nature does things and then you'll have that example. The orderliness of the universe and the inter-relation of all natural laws; the fixation of all the stars and planets in the immovable relationship between one another.

Isn't it the most marvelous thing? To know that astronomers can sit down and with a pencil and a few pieces of paper, predetermine hundreds of years in advance the exact relationship of given planets and stars right where they'll be with relationship to one another in advance. And you know they couldn't do that if there was not a purpose a plan under which we're working. We want to find out what that purpose is as it relates to us as individuals.

That's why you're in this course; that's why I'm teaching you. I'm giving you that little bit that I've picked up from life and from the experiences of men and from my own experience; so that you will learn how to adjust yourself to the laws of nature; in order that you may use those laws instead of allowing yourself to be abused by your neglect in using them.

To me one of the most horrible things to contemplate is the possible cessation of natural laws. Imagine all of the chaos, all of the stars and planets running together; why they'd make the h-bomb look like a firecracker. If nature allowed her laws to be suspended but she doesn't do that, she has very definite laws to go by and you'll find if you check these seventeen principles, they check perfectly with all of the laws of nature.

You get over to that principle of going the extra mile you'll find that nature is profound in her application of the principle of going the extra mile. When she produces blooms on the trees, she doesn't produce just enough to fill the tree, she produces enough to take care of all of the damages of the winds and storms. When she produces fish in the seas, she doesn't just produce enough to perpetuate the fish, she produces enough to feed the bullfrogs and the snakes and the alligators and all the other things and still have enough left to carry out her purpose.

She has an abundance of things; over-abundance. And also she forces man to go the extra mile or else he'll perish. He would perish in one season if he didn't go the extra mile. If nature didn't compensate a man when he goes out and puts a grain of wheat in the ground by giving him back five hundred grains to compensate him for his intelligence, why we'd starve to death in one season.

If you do your part, nature does her part and she does it in abundance; in abundance; in super-abundance. And one of the strange things about nature is that if you keep your mind focused on the positive side of life, it becomes greater than the negative side; always does that. If you keep your mind on the positive side, it becomes greater than all of the negatives that may try to penetrate your mind and influence your life.

Look around and you'll find examples, living examples all around you of people that you want to emulate and people you do not want to emulate, people that are failing and you'll be able to tell why they're failing. I dare say, from this time on, you'll be able to use this philosophy as a measuring stick and wherever you find a success or a failure you'll be able to lay your finger right on the cause of it; right on it and that includes you too.

End of Volume 1

Bonus – Volume 2

Chapter 1 - The First Premise

First of all, the first premise is that the mastermind principle is the medium through which one may procure the full benefits of the experience, the training, the education and the specialized knowledge and influence of others as completely as if their minds were in reality one's own.

Isn't that a marvelous thing to contemplate? That whatever it is that you lack in education or in knowledge or influence, you can always obtain it through somebody who has it. The exchange of favors, the exchange of knowledge is one of the greatest exchanges in the world. It's a very nice thing to engage in the business where the exchange of money makes you a profit but I would a whole lot rather exchange ideas with somebody; give a man an idea that he didn't have before and receive in return one that I didn't have and I would do it and make it an exchange of money.

You of course know that Thomas A. Edison was perhaps the greatest inventor the world has ever known. He was dealing all the time with many of the sciences and yet he knew nothing at all about any of the sciences. You'd say it would be impossible for a man to succeed in any undertaking unless he were educated in that field.

I was astounded when I first talked to Andrew Carnegie, to hear him say that he personally didn't know anything about the making or the marketing of steel. And I was so astounded at that statement that I said to Mr. Carnegie, "Well, jusr what is your part in this job here? What part do you play?" Well, he said, "I'll tell you the part that I play. My job is to keep the members of my mastermind alliance, working in a state of perfect harmony."

And I said, "Is that all you have to do?" He said, "Well, have you ever tried to get any two people to agree on anything for three minutes in succession in your life?" I said, "Well, I don't know that I have."

Well he said, "You try it someday and see just what kind of job it is. To get people to work together in the spirit of harmony is one of the greatest of human achievements."

And then Mr. Carnegie went on to breakdown his mastermind group to describe each one individually to tell what part he played, One was his metallurgist, one was this Chief Chemist, one was his plant works Manager and one was his Legal Adviser, one was the Chief of his Financial Staff, and so on down the line, of over 20 of those men working together whose combined education, experience and knowledge constituted all there was known about the making and the marketing of steel at that time.

And Mr. Carnegie says it wasn't necessary for him to know about it, he had men all around him who did understand the making and the marketing of steel and that was his job to keep them working in perfect harmony.

Chapter 2 – The Second Premise

And the second premise, an active alliance of two or more minds in a spirit of perfect harmony for the attainment of a common objective stimulates each individual mind to a higher degree of courage, than that which is ordinarily experienced and prepares the way for that state of mind known as faith. You know driving an automobile every so often the battery runs down and you have to do something about it. You come out some morning and you step on the starter, nothing happens.

I know people who could get out of bed in the morning do the same thing and nothing happens except they feel badly. They don't want to put on their shoes, they don't want to get dressed and they don't even want to eat breakfast. Now, what do they need?

They need the batteries charged, of course and they have to have a source for doing it. It's a mighty fine thing if a man man gets up in the morning and feeling like that and if he can have a little talk with his wife, for instance, and she's a good coordinator and she helps to charge his batteries.

Chances are when he comes home that night, he will come home with all of the rabbits' skins that he went out to get.

Chapter 3 – The Third Premise

The third premise, a mastermind alliance properly conducted stimulates each mind in the alliance to move with enthusiasm, personal initiative, imagination and courage to a degree far above that which the individual experiences when moving without such an alliance.

In my own early beginning, I had a mastermind alliance of three people. I had an alliance with Mr. Carnegie and with my stepmother and we through three people nursed this philosophy through the stages, when everybody else was laughing at me and making fun of me, for undertaking to serve the richest man in the world for 20 years, without any compensation. And there was a whole lot of logic to what they were saying because at that time, I wasn't getting very much compensation out of it in the way of money at least. There came a time however when the laughing was on the other side of the fence but that took a long time and there was plenty of blood and tears shed I'll assure before I got to the point to which I could laugh back when the people laughed at me.

But the relationship between we, three people, my stepmother and Mr. Carnegie and myself enabled me to offset all of this fun-making that was thrown at me by my relatives, my friends and everybody who knew what I was engaged in. There are times, you know, when if you undertake anything above mediocrity, you're going to meet with opposition, you're going to meet with people who charge you and make fun at you and most of them will be right close to you, some of them perhaps would even be your own relatives.

You need some source to which you can turn when you're going to aim above the mediocrity to get your battery charged and to keep it charged so that you won't quit when the going is hard. I hope so you won't pay any attention when somebody criticizes you.

You know, criticism falls on my back just like water off a ducks back or more than that like a bullet off a rhinoceros' hide. I am immune, absolutely immune to all forms of criticism. Whether it's friendly or unfriendly and it makes no difference to me whatsoever, I'm just immune to it. That's all. And I became immune because of my relationship with certain people through whom I built up an immunity under my mastermind alliance.

If it had not been for the relationship with my stepmother and Mr. Carnegie, I wouldn't be standing here talking to you folks tonight and that you wouldn't be here the students in this philosophy, and this philosophy would not be spread all over the world helping millions of people. Because I had a million opportunities to quit, at least a million opportunities and every one of them looked very alluring and almost sometimes, it seemed as if I were stupid if I didn't quit.

But this marvelous relationship I could always go back to Mr. Carnegie. I could always run into my stepmother and we could sit down and have a little chat and she would say, "Stand by your guns. You'll come back up on top. I know you will."

She once said, at the times when I didn't have two nickels to rub together, as my enemies were saying, she once said that, "You are going to be the richest member of the Hill family far and away. I know it. I can see it in the future." Well, if you would take all of my riches and put them together, I suspect that I have more riches, and all of my relatives put together for 3 generations back on both sides of the house. That's true.

And my stepmother could see that. She could see what I was doing and was bound to make me rich and I'm not and I don't have reference alone to monetary riches, I have reference to those higher and broader riches, that you find when you get to where you can render service to so many people.

Chapter 4 – The Fourth Premise

And the fourth premise, to be effective a mastermind alliance must be active. It must be active. You can't just formulize with somebody and say, "That's it. We've got it." I'm lined up with this person, that person, we've got a mastermind alliance; no, you're got absolutely nothing until you become active. Every member of the alliance, you've got to step right in there and then start pitching, mentally, spiritually, physically, financially, every way that's necessary. But they must engage in pursuit of a definite purpose and they must move with perfect harmony.

Do you know difference between perfect harmony and ordinary harmony? Do you know what it is? How many of you don't know the difference between perfect harmony and ordinary harmony? How many of you have never had a relationship of perfect harmony with anybody? I'll tell you the truth. I suspect that if I have had more harmonious relationships with about so many people, maybe more people than any person living today. I don't have any question about that.

But I would also tell you that perfect harmony in relationships is about the rarest thing in the world, and I think I could count on the fingers of my two hands, all of the people that I now know that I have a relationship of perfect harmony. I have speaking acquaintances and I like speaking with friends with a lot of people but that's not perfect harmony.

I have working alliances with a lot of people, that's not perfect harmony. Perfect harmony consists only when your relationship to the other person, except that if he wants everything you have, you're willing to turn it over to them. Now, it takes a lot of unselfishness to put yourself in that same alliance.

Mr. Carnegie, stressed time and time again, the importance of this relationship of perfect harmony because he said, "If you don't have perfect harmony in your mastermind alliance, it's not the mastermind alliance after all, it's just cooperation or a coordination of effort."

Without this aspect of harmony, the alliance maybe nothing more than ordinary cooperation or friendly coordination of effort, the mastermind gives one full access to the spiritual powers of the other members of the alliance. I want you to underscore that part in your notes.

The mastermind gives one full access to the spiritual powers of the other members of his alliance. I'm not talking now about just the mental powers or the financial powers but the spiritual powers. The feelings that you have when you begin to establish permanency in your mastermind relationship is going to be probably one of the most outstanding and pleasant experiences of your entire life.

When you're engaged in a mastermind activity, I will tell you that you have so much faith, you can do anything that you start out to do and you can start anything you need to do. You have no doubts, you have no fears, you have no limitations and that's a marvelous frame of mind to be at.

Chapter 5 – The Fifth Premise

And the 6th premise...

Yes, I just want to know if you are following me. It is the 5th.

It is a matter of established record that all individual successes based upon any kind of achievement above mediocrity are attained through the mastermind principle and not by individual effort alone.

Just imagine how little you could accomplish if you didn't have the cooperation of other people, suppose that you're in a profession, suppose you're a dentist, you're a lawyer or a doctor or naturopath or anybody in the profession. And suppose that you didn't understand how to convert each one of your clients, or patients into a salesman for yourself, imagine how long it would take to build up a clientele or a following. The outstanding professional men understand how to make a salesman out of every person that they serve and they do it all by indirectly, they don't go about it directly. They do it by going the extra mile, by going out of their way to give unusual service but they do make salesmen out of all their clients.

Most successes are the result of personal power and personal power of sufficient proportions to enable one to arise above mediocrity is not possible without the application of the mastermind principle.

Chapter 6 - Thinking Positive During the Great Depression

Now, during the first term of Franklin D. Roosevelt, in the Whitehouse, I had the privilege of working with him, as a Confidential Adviser and it was I who laid out the skeleton of the propaganda plan that took the words 'business depression' out of the headlines of the papers, and substituted in their stead 'business recovery'. Those of who would remember what happened on that Black Sunday when we had a meeting down at the Whitehouse and the banks were closed the following Monday morning.

Will remember how, what a stampede there was in this country. People were lined up in front of banks all over the country to withdraw up their deposits. They were scared to death, they had lost confidence in their country, in their banks and themselves and everybody else. I suppose they still had some confidence in God but they didn't show much signs of it. It was a scary time I tell you and that we sat down there and worked up a skeleton of a plan of procedure that created one of the most outstanding applications of the mastermind that this nation has ever seen and I doubt that if any nation out there has ever been able to equal.

Because it was only a matter of weeks until we had picked up all that spirit of fear out of people. It was only a matter of days until salesman on the road, who had run out of funds, who couldn't get money, who were laughing about it and not in any way scared about it. My own funds were close to gone, I had no money, none at all. Yes, actually I did have some. I must tell you, this is funny. I got very smart when I saw all this was coming and I went down to the bank and got a $1,000-bill. Well I might just as well as had only ten cents, nobody could change it. It was not worth a nickel, not a nickel. But I wasn't scared because everybody else was in the same boat as I was in, but something had to be done about it and Franklin D. Roosevelt was a great leader. He had great imagination. He had great courage.

And here is what we did, first of all, we got both Houses of Congress working in harmony with the President, the first time in the history of this nation that both Houses of Congress Democrats and Republicans alike, got behind the President and forgot about what their political face happened to be. In other words, there were no democrats, there were no republicans, they were just Americans down there backing the president everything he needed in order to stop that stampede of fear.

I had never seen anything equal to it in my life. I never hope to see it again. I would wish I could but I don't hope to. Of course it was a great emergency on and something had to be done about it. The majority of the newspapers published everywhere, "Everything is set up." The newspapers published that. They gave it marvelous space.

And then the radio station operators. They gave us marvelous space despite their political belief, and the churches, all of them, all, that was the most beautiful thing I've ever seen in this country. The Catholics and Protestants, Jews and Gentiles, and all of the rest, pulling together as Americans. I want to tell you, that was a wonderful time. It was a wonderful time.

What a wonderful thing it was. They all got behind the President. Every one of them made some sort of a contribution towards re-establishing faith in the people of this country. But during these hectic days, I want to tell you there was any doubt in the minds of the majority of the people. I don't know. I didn't come into contact with anybody who didn't think that Mr. Roosevelt was the only man, the finest man that could possibly have handled that chaotic condition.

And don't get me wrong politically, I am just talking about a great man who did a great job at a time when it was needed to be done, and he did it because he had mastermind alliances out there that were unbeatable.

Chapter 7 – Types of Alliances

Now let's pick up the different kinds of master mind alliances you may have. First of all, there are alliances of purely social or personal reasons, consisting of one's relatives, friends, and religious advisers; where no material gain is sought.

The most important of this type is the mastermind alliance which may exist between the man and his wife. I couldn't emphasize if I were brilliant or if I had the great magnetic powers, I couldn't over-emphasize the importance to you who are married, of going to work immediately and re-dedicating that marriage to a mastermind alliance based upon these lessons tonight.

It will bring joy into your alliance that you never dreamed of. It will bring success into your life that you never dreamed of. It will bring health into your life that you never dreamed of. It's a perfectly marvelous thing when the real mastermind alliance exists between a man and his wife. I don't know of anything its' equal.

And then there are alliances for business or professional advancement consisting of individuals who have a personal motive of a material or a financial nature connected with the object of their alliances.

I imagine that the majority of you who are in this class now will be forming your first mastermind alliances for purely economic or financial advancement reasons, and that's perfectly legitimate. That's one of the reasons why you're taking this course.

You want to improve your economic and financial condition and you should start in immediately now to form a mastermind alliance for that purpose and if you only have to begin with only one person, that's alright. Start up with one; and then look around until the two of you can select a third. Now, you can't select another one by yourself but the two of you. When you go to select the third one, be sure that the second one that you already selected is in accord. You understand that, that's important.

And then when you go to select the fourth, the three of you then will agree on the fourth and then you'll go over the matter very carefully before you make him a member of the alliance. And then when you go to select the fifth, the four of you will select the fifth.

You see, in the mastermind alliance, there's no such thing as one person dominating except in this aspect that, generally speaking, one person is the leader. He is the coordinator and the leader but he in no way undertakes to dominate his associates, because the very moment you start to dominate anybody, you find resistance and rebellions, even though it's not open rebellion, it's rebellion nevertheless. And in the mastermind alliance is supposed to be one continuous spirit of perfect harmony while you move and act as if you are only one mind.

The American system of free enterprise is another example of efficiency through the mastermind principle. This system is the envy of the world because it has raised the standard of living of the American people to an all-time high level and that despite the fact that there's not perfect harmony. But there is motive; there is motive in the American system of free enterprise, to inspire every individual to do his best. There is a motive there, and this definitely more and more industry and business is coming to understand that they can go to step further and then instead of just having cooperation or coordination of effort between management and the workers, that they can have the mastermind of friendship by sharing the management of problems, by sharing profits, by sharing everything.

And however, as I have been successful on the influence in any business to adapt that policy and the business has to make more money than it's ever made before and the employees receive more wages and everybody is happy.

Chapter 8 – General Instructions – Qualities for Master Mind Members

General instructions for the forming and the maintenance of a mastermind alliance.

First, adopt the definite purpose as an objective to be attained by the alliance choosing every individual member whose education, experience and influence are such as to make them of the greatest value in achieving the purpose. A lot of times, I ask by my students, "What is the most favorable number for a mastermind alliance? And how do you go about selecting the right type of people for you mastermind alliance?" And the nearest answer that I can give you that, is the procedure is exactly the same as if you're starting into the business and you were choosing employees. What kind of employee would you choose?

Marvelous! That's even sparks for long. Wonderful! Wonderful! **Dependability** at the top of the list. If the person is not dependable, I don't want any part of him in a business transaction. No part of him, no matter how brilliant he may be, no matter how well-educated he may be, and the more educated he is, the more dangerous he may be if he's not dependable. And if he's not loyal, I would say the same thing. If an individual is not loyal to whom he owes **loyalty**, then to me he has no character and I want no part of him.

Dependability and loyalty and then after that comes what? Ability to do the job. Ability, notice where I place ability, down the third place. I am not interested in a man's ability until I have found out found out that he's dependable and is loyal. And then what would you say came after that in my category, in my book of rules. Number 4, **positive mental attitude**, of course. What good is a negative wet blanket around you, why you could pay him to stay away and then be ahead of the game.

And number 5, what would that be? **Going the extra mile**, that is right. And number 6, what would you say that is? **Applied faith**.

Now, let me tell you, when you find people that come up to all of those 6 traits I want to tell you, you've really found somebody. You're in the presence of royalty. Some businesses like if you're running a peanut stand, maybe you need only one person, but if you're running a chain of peanut stands, you might need 100 persons. And then as for the qualifications of a mastermind alliance, first of all, take those 6 points that I gave you and they are the qualifications. They are the qualifications where you're masterminding; there must be dependability, there must be loyalty, there must be ability, must be positive mental attitude, must be able to willing to go to an extra mile, applied faith. Now, there you are if you want to know what's the qualifications of your mastermind alliance, there it is.

And don't settle for anything less, if you find the man that has 5 of those but doesn't have all 6 of them, you better beware before you start because they are all essential in the mastermind relationship. You can check very carefully to see that that's true. You couldn't find a perfect harmony unless you are working with somebody who checks 100% on all of those 6 points. You just couldn't have a mastermind alliance. You might have a working arrangement like so many people do, but it wouldn't embrace all of those potential values of the mastermind.

Next, determine what appropriate benefit each member may receive in return for his cooperation in this alliance, and remember ladies and gentlemen, nobody ever does anything for nothing. No, they never do. You say, when you give love to somebody, you don't have to get anything out of that? You don't do that for nothing? Well, let me tell you something. You get plenty out of that, because you have the privilege of loving, it's a great privilege and even though, the love is not returned, you still have had the benefit of that state of mind known as love and you have enjoyed that development and growth as a result of it. There's no such thing or something for nothing.

Nobody works without some sort of compensation, maybe it's a different sort of compensation so don't expect that your mastermind allies are going to join you and help you make a fortune without you having to do anything unless they are equally participating in the benefits that come out of that mastermind alliance.

Now, there's the criteria and by which you must go. They must approximately, each individual must approximately benefit equally with yourself, whether it's a monetary benefit or a happiness or piece of mind benefit, social benefits or whatever that type happens to be. Never ask anybody to do anything if you want to be sure of his doing it, unless you give him an adequate motive for doing it. If I went down to the bank and wanted to borrow $10,000, what would be an adequate motive for the bank lending me that money? Two motives, all of them under the heading of the desire for financial gains. Now, the bank would want to loan me as much money as I can take away if I could give them three for one security, or collateral. They want collateral and they want the profit on that loan, that's what they are in business for.

There are other transactions not based on monetary motives. There's this guy and the man actually asks the girl to marry him, what's the motive there?

Audience: Love.

Sometimes [laughs]. Theoretically love, yes.

Audience: Money.

[laughs] Well isn't this interesting. Listen to these things. I bet all of the people sitting there, everyone have a different idea or definition of what's the motive is when a man actually asks the girl to marry then she accepts. Why does she accept? [Laughs].

I want to tell you that when my father brought my stepmother home, he was just a farmer and he never had on a white shirt or a tie. He was afraid of white shirts and ties. He wore a blue cotton shirts and my stepmother was a college women. She was well-educated and they were as different as the North Pole and the South Pole, and I wondered all my life until one day, just how he had been able to sell himself to her. Of course she cleaned him up and put a white shirt on him and make him look like somebody but nevertheless, it took her a little while to do it. And she finally got him into the money and he became quite an outstanding man.

And at that point, I said to her one day, "How in the world did my father"; I remember what he looked like and what he talked like; he used the Queen's English. I've seen him coming and I've done my duty and all that sort of thing, and then I started to think, I said,

"How in the world did he ever sell himself to you, what was the motive?"

She said, "Well, I'll tell you. First of all, I recognized that he had good blood in his veins and possibilities and I believed that I could bring them out." And she did bring them out.

If you had a definite major purpose and knew exactly what you wanted to do, had a mastermind alliance of people that could help you do it and then had sufficient faith to keep you going while you did it, don't you see that would be about all you would need? Why then do we need the fourteen additional principles do you suppose. Well, I tell you why. We need fourteen additional principles to induce you to make use of these three.

You need personal initiative. You need imagination. You need enthusiasm. In other words, this philosophy is something like baking a cake. When you go to bake a cake, you don't put in just one ingredient, you put in a pinch of this and a pinch of that and a dash of the other thing, and then you put it in the stove and bake it and if you took out any one of those ingredients you wouldn't have the same kind of a cake. And this is same way with this philosophy, you can't leave out any one of these seventeen principles, or it's like if you start picking a link out of a chain, you wouldn't have a chain anymore, you have two parts of a chain and not a whole chain.

And these are the fourteen principles or supporting principles of these three.

Chapter 9 – Supporting Principles

Faith is a state of mind that has been called the mainspring of the soul to which one's aims, desires, plans and purposes maybe translated into their physical or financial equivalent. And here are the fundamentals of faith, now, when we speak of **applied faith**, ladies and gentlemen, we're talking about something far different from just mere belief. Applied, the word applied means what? Action, that's the action part of faith. And then without action, faith is nothing but just daydreaming.

And there a lot of people who believe in things but they don't do anything about them. They are engaging only in daydreaming. Applied faith is an active faith. Now, the fundamentals of faith are first of all, definitely it's a purpose supported by personal initiative and action. Action, action – the more action, the better. That means continuous action. Not only on your part but on the part of those that may be cooperating with you or may be mastermind allies of yours.

And next, **a positive mind**, free from all the negatives such as fear, envy, hatred, jealousy and greed is essential. Mental attitude determines the effectiveness of faith. Mental attitude, did you know that that is a fact? The frame of mind that you're in when you go to pray determines what happens as a result of that prayer. There's no two ways about that, you can test that yourself to find out, I have no doubt you have.

I have no doubt that you have had the experiences that I had of sending out prayers and didn't produce anything but a negative result. You have had that experience, haven't you? How many of you had that experience? Oh! Come on, be modest. You suppose that everyone didn't have that experience at one time or another? I would have to tell you that when you go to prayer, unless you have such absolute faith that whatever you are going after, that you are going to acquire, you can see it in advance in your possession before you start asking for it; the chances are the effect of your prayer is going to be negative.

And next, **a mastermind alliance with one or more people who radiate courage based on faith** and are suited mentally and spiritually, to ones' need in carrying out the given purpose. I'm talking to you now about the elements or the constituent parts or the premises that go into the business of applied faith.

And next, recognition of the fact that every adversity carries within it the seed of an equivalent benefit and temporary defeat is not failure until it has been accepted as such. You know why the majority of people fall down in connection with their application of faith; it's when they're defeated when they begin to accept that defeat as being something that they can't do anything about.

And instead of beginning immediately to search out seeking the seed of an equivalent benefit that's been in every defeat, they'd become moody and broody, they'd become discouraged, they build up inferiority complexes, instead of reversing that order and using that defeat as stuff nothing more than temporary and making another effort.

Next is a habit of affirming ones' definite major purpose in the form of a prayer at least once daily.

The subconscious mind will only be able to know what you tell it or what you allow other people to tell it or what you allow the circumstances of life to tell it, and it doesn't know the difference between the lie and the truth and it doesn't know the difference between a penny and a million dollars. It accepts the things that you send over, and if you send over predominating thoughts on poverty and ill heath and failure, well, that's exactly what you'll get. No matter how much faith that you may have later on, you'll find out that the subconscious response to the mental attitude that you're maintaining during the day. And it's necessary for you to affirm over and over again the objects that you're going to attain in life, until you educate your subconscious mind to attract automatically to you the things that you're aiming to attain in life.

You'll find that your mind is like an electromagnet and once you charge it, and put a clear picture of what you want, it will attract to you from the highways and the byways, the things that you need to carry out that purpose.

And next, recognition of the existence of Infinite Intelligence that gives order in the list of the entire universe, that the individual (you) that is, is a minute expression of this Intelligence and as such, you, the individual, your mind has no limitations except those accepted or set up in your own mind.

Your mind has no limitations whatsoever, except those that you allow to be established there or that you deliberately set up in your own mind or accept. Now that's a pretty broad statement, isn't it? But the achievements of men like Mr. Edison and Mr. Ford and Mr. Carnegie and Napoleon Hill, if you please, certainly definitely supports the idea that there is no limitation except that which you set up in your own mind and if I had ever waivered one second, from the time that I started with Mr. Carnegie up until the time I gave this philosophy to the world; if I had ever waivered for one second in my belief that I would do that, I would never have done it.

How did I have to do it? Do you have any idea what played the strongest part in what I've achieved? It wasn't that I was brilliant. I have no more brilliancy than the average person. No more intelligence than the average person. But there was something in there was responsible for it.

In other words, I believe that I could do and I never stopped believing it, the harder the going was, the more I believed that I would do it. And I want to tell you that if you can take that attitude towards yourself, if you can tell yourself over on the side of yourself so to speak, when you're overtaken by adversity, when people are guessing, if you can do that. If you would stand by yourself and not go over against yourself, then you're using applied faith and you've got to do that. You know, there are testing times with people. Have you ever thought of that?

Nobody is permitted to attain a high state in life and stay there without being tested. Anymore than anybody is allowed to go into a well-managed business and go up to a high position and stay there without ever being tested with lower position step-by-step until he earns the right to be up on top.

I don't know how the creator runs his business entirely but I can see – I can catch a pretty good idea of how He does it by observing that part of what I can understand, of course there's much more that I can't understand. But I can see definitely that he allows nobody to attain to a highest state in life without severe testings.

One of the most outstanding things that I found in my research was that the men of great achievement in all parts of life back down through the ages were great only in proportion as they had been defeated and thus they had met with great opposition. That's the outstanding thing, it couldn't have been a coincidence that every one of these outstanding men was great in proportion exactly as he had been small and as he had been opposed and as he had had to struggle.

I used to tell of my early struggles and tell of some of my defeats and my business partners would say, "It wasn't a good idea." I still think it's a good idea. I think it's a fine idea, because if you only knew the amount of major defeats that I met with but still kept my head above water and still I was able to deliver this philosophy, you'd say, that if you can do it, I can do it too. And that's the only reason of course that I ever spoke of it.

Chapter 10 – Infinite Intelligence

The habit of affirming your definite major purpose in the form of a prayer at least daily and the recognition of Infinite Intelligence.

I don't mind what terms you use. You can call that God, or you can call Jehovah or you can call that Buddha or you can call that Mohammad, anything you want to. No matter what you call it, we're all part of the first cause. There aren't two first cause. This is only one. There couldn't be two. There's one first cause that's responsible for this great universe we're living in, for you and for me and for everything that's in the universe.

I call it Infinite Intelligence because I have students of all faiths and all religions all over the world as my students, and the Infinite Intelligence happens to be a sort of a neutral in-between term that nobody can object you. Nobody at all, but unless you not only believe in that and that unless you can prove it to yourself, unless you can absolutely put down on paper evidence that there is a first cause that you can draw on, you're not going to be able to make the fullest use of applied faith.

One of my students asked me one day about my concept of God, he asked if my concept of Infinite Intelligence, did I just mean the same thing as God and I said "Yes I do." Well he said, "can you prove the existence of your concept of God?' I said, "Well, everything in the universe is the finest of evidence of the existence of God, because of the orderliness of the universe. Everything is orderly from the electrons and protons of the smallest parts of matter, all up to the largest sun that floats to the heavens; everything is in orderliness, no chaos, and no running together of the planets." There is more evidence of a first cause than anything that I know of.

And if you don't believe that, if you don't accept it, if you don't see it, you don't feel then you don't know that, then you won't know that you are a small part of that Infinite Intelligence expressing through your brain. And once you recognize that, then you recognize the truth of what I said that your only limitations are those that you set up in your own mind or permit somebody to set up there or circumstances to establish for you.

Chapter 11 – Overcoming Adversity

Next, careful inventory of your past defeats and adversities from which it becomes obvious that all such experiences do carry the seed of an equivalent benefit. Now, just to hear me say, that every adversity carries within it the seed of an equivalent benefit; wouldn't mean a thing in the world to you; unless I made application of it and gave you illustration after illustration; unless you examined enough illustrations into your own experience to see that it always works out that way. That's why I want you to examine these adversities that come to you.

Do you know that often times, that your adversities are your greatest blessings? Do you have any idea about that the greatest blessing that ever came into my life? Those of you who know considerable about me will know, well do you have any idea about what it was? Of course, it was the loss of my mother.

And ordinarily you would say that would be the greatest catastrophe that can overtake a child would be to lose his mother at the age of nine years. Why do I say that was the greatest blessing? Because it brought me a new mother to take her place who was responsible for everything that I've achieved, everything that I shall achieve, very largely responsible at least. And without her influence, I'd still be up there fighting rattlesnakes and drinking mountain liquor and fighting feuds. Well, my relatives still are doing that same thing. No reason to expect that I wouldn't be.

I've had a lot of other adversities and I want to tell you that without the some twenty major adversities I've gone through, will I would never been able to approve the soundness of this philosophy and that there is a seed of an equivalent benefit in every adversity.

Can you imagine any worst adversity coming to a man than to walk down to the hospital and to be informed that his son was born without any sign of any ears? That he would be deaf dumb and mute all of his life? Can imagine any worse adversity than that? I will always be thankful that it happened because by my contact with Intimate Intelligence, he was improvised with a hearing system of some sort that give him 65% of his normal hearing and with a hearing aid, 100%. He learned to live a normal life and I got the greatest demonstration of my entire experience of the power of faith. I couldn't have gotten it any other way. I couldn't have gotten it second hand; I had to get it first hand.

I never accepted that the depiction of that child not even before I saw him, not even after I saw him. I never accepted it. He had relatively accepted it. They wanted to put him in the school of the underprivileged, where he would learn the sign language, learn lip-reading. I didn't want him to know there were such things. But when he got up to the age where he got to go to school, I had to fight with the school authorities every year just as regular as the time came around, they wanted to send him over to the school for underprivileged children where he would mix with the other children and see that they were afflicted.

I didn't want him to know there were such things and I told him from the very beginning that his not having any ears was a great blessing and he believed it, and it turned out to be because people took compassion on him. They did things for him that they would not have done otherwise. He got a job as a salesman for the Saturday Evening Post and he lead every salesman throughout the United States.

Often times, he would go out with a $5 worth of merchandise and come back with $10 in cash. He did that many times. People would look at him and say "well that poor little fellow with no ears is out selling papers, I guess his parents are poor". They would give him a dollar bill and instead of him giving them back 95 cents in change, instead they would say, "You just keep that." And very often, he would get a dollar a piece for The Saturday Evening Post.

Not at all conscious today of any affliction, he's living a perfectly normal life because I taught him that an affliction; any kind of an affliction can be transmuted into a benefit.

Well, that's an outstanding thing, isn't it? To consider that, that is true, but it is true. Well, as I said, you just hearing me say that won't mean a thing in the world unless you begin to look around in your own experiences, take inventory and watch what happens in the future. That will be some things happen to you in the future and they will be unpleasant and they will come to me too.

But I can tell about what I am going to do when something unpleasant happens to me, I'm going to immediately transmute it into something pleasant immediately and then I'm still talking about the fundamentals of faith.

Chapter 12 – Self-Respect

Self-respect expressed through harmony with one's own conscience; it's certainly an important factor in applied faith. Self-respect expressed through harmony with one's own conscience. Isn't it a marvelous thing that the creator set up a judge advocate that tells you the right thing and the wrong thing to do? Isn't that a marvelous thing? You don't have to ask anything about what's right or wrong, your own conscience does it, unless you convert into a conspirator instead of a cooperator by choking it off and not responding to it as so many people do.

Your conscience can be not only a guide but it can also be corrupted towards a conspirator to help you cover up your meanness and a lot of people use it for just that purpose too. Believe me, they have it choked off. If that weren't true there wouldn't be so many boots loose in the world today and talking plans of starting bigger and better wars. They have no conscience. They killed off their conscience. But conscience is a marvelous thing.

And next to create a mental attitude, favorable for the expression of faith. Now, here is what you do, first of all, know what you want and determine what you have to give in return for it. Know what you want in life, and I mean not only in your major purpose but in your minor purposes. What kind of a house you want to live in? What kind of a car you want to drive? What kind of wardrobe you want? What kind of education you want your children to have? What kind of a present you're going to buy your wife for her birthday? And you better be sure to buy her one every time if you want to keep on good terms with her. What kind of a cake you're going to bake your husband in his birthday? And you better make it a good one.

Didn't you know, ladies and gentlemen, that is you married ladies and gentlemen, did you know it's not the big things in the relationship between a man and his wife that counts, it's the little niceties, the little things that counts.

Well, it's the little niceties, the little things. The little things that my wife cooks up for me. Now, I don't mean in food but the little parties, the little visits, and the little trips she cooks up for me when I'm home. And they come up to so much in one way and yet in another way, they are very sentimental and keep that relationship alive that keeps what we had before we were married. We're still courting each other. I think I have more to do in the courting job now than ever, after all I not only have her but I have to keep her. (laughs)

Well I have a lot of fun with these off the cuff remarks but you know you don't find these in my notes at all, but I just know that these are very super-intimate things that make joy in my life and would likely be just as acceptable in your life too. I know it's the little things in your life that makes the difference between happiness and unhappiness.

And next, when you affirm the object of your desires, through prayer, let your imagination see yourself already in possession on the things that you're going at.

You might say, that takes a lot of willpower and determination but if you keep at it, you'll find this is not so hard to do. In the first place, it's easy for me to do that because I never go after anything but I haven't first sold myself thoroughly on the idea that I not only have the right to get it but I am going to earn that right by giving something in return and that's the best salesmanship in the world.

When you go out to sell a person an idea or some merchandize or services, if you know positively that you're going to give him his money's worth first and more before you start; it does something to you that enable you to do something to him that enables him in return to do something for you. It's the very apex of master salesmanship.

You know I said this, ladies and gentlemen, several times and at the risk of being boresome to you, I'm going to repeat, that if you want your prayers to be effective, don't wait until the time of need to utter them. Do that habit of prayer when you don't need anything and what do you pray for then? For what you already have. You give gratitude for what already have, don't you?

Wouldn't that be an interesting thing if I give you a lesson assignment right now to write down before the night before you go to bed tonight, everything that you have in this world to be thankful for? And I'm giving you that assignment, everyone of you and I want you to carry it out. This is going to be among the surprises of your life. You may have a lot of things you don't want but you have a lot of things you do want. Write down all these then and express gratitude that you have these things that you love. And you certainly can start with the fact that you are associated here in a country, where you have freedom of speech, freedom of action, freedom of thought and freedom of opportunity. Certainly that would head the list; there's another countries who don't have that much.

And then you could come on down from that and put all the things that you have gratefulness for and then start in the expressing of gratitude every night and everyday. Keep your mind open for guidance from within.

Now, what do I mean by that do you suppose? Yes, hunches, you get hunches, don't be (what is the word I'm going to use?) disrespectful [laughs]. Don't be disrespectful of hunches treat them with civility, examine them and you may find that some of these very unusual hunches that will come are bringing you messages that you need to get you over the hump in whatever it is that you're doing.

And when you are inspired by hunches to move on some plan created by your imagination, which leads in the direction of that which you desire, accept the plan and act upon it at once. And remember always there can be no such state of mind as faith without appropriate action. Faith without deeds is dead.

When you're overtaken by defeat as you may be many times, remember that your faith may be tested many times and your defeat maybe only one of your testing times. Isn't that an outstanding and an encouraging thing to recognize that when you're meeting with defeat, that probably in the eyes of your creator, you're only being tested to see whether you're a man or a worm. And believe me we all go through those testing times.

And the ones that survive these tests and come out on top with an abiding faith are the ones that become truly great in life. I don't think there's any doubt in the world, but it's part of the creator's plan to see that everybody that will amount to anything above mediocrity must pay the price of undergoing test after test as to his faith. I don't think there's any doubt about that. I see evidence everywhere that that's true.

Any negative state of mind will destroy the power of faith and result in a negative climate. Your state of mind is everything. Why do you suppose that in my notes here, you notice that I have underscored, <u>your state of mind is everything.</u> I underscored for emphasis and why do you suppose I want to emphasize that statement?

That's right. That's the only thing you have control over. The only thing in this world that you have control over is your state of mind and certainly that connotes, the fact that the Creator intended that to be the most important asset that you have and it is because with the use of that mind, you can project it into any objective or to the attainment of any end you choose. Your education, your background, your nationality, your creed has nothing whatsoever to do with your ability to achieve. It's the state of mind that you maintain, that's the thing that determines how and what and when you will achieve.

To me, that's the most profound thing in all of the knowledge of mankind. The most profound of all knowledge, is the fact that the humblest person can take possession of his own mind, he can color it anyway he chooses, he can project it into high places or into the gutter. He can make it a success or he can make it a failure, just a change of his mental attitude can change him from success to failure almost instantly.

Chapter 13 – Burning Desire

A burning desire is the sort of material of which faith is created. Do you know what a burning desire is?

That's right, obsessional desire, and obsessional means the desire that takes possession of you and obsesses you. And there are a lot of desires in the world but they're not burning desires and they're not obsessional desires, and most people in their whole life never express or never experience an obsessional desire for anything.

We start up with hopes not too definite but faint hopes and wishing. We wish for – everybody wishes for a lot of money without having to work for it and maybe not everybody but of course my students know, but a lot of people do. Most people, I have to say, wish for thing, wish for the Cadillac when they're driving the Ford. If you want a Cadillac car and you make up your mind to have it, get out and see that the jobs that you're holding and see that you put into it that which entitles you to the Cadillac car. But if you don't want a Cadillac car, then chances are that and you will likely drive a Ford for the rest of your life.

You have to want things. You have to want them with a burning desire and then you have to do something about that burning desire. What is it?

Action! You've got to start in right where you stand showing that you do have faith in your abilities. Start right away you stand with action. Here are a lot of examples with the men of achievements. I'm not going to go over them. You know them, but there is one down here that I particularly want to call your attention to, and she's Helen Keller, who believed that she would learn to talk despite the fact that she had lost the use of her speech, her sight and her hearing. Can you imagine that? Lost the use early in life, her speech, her sight and her hearing. She couldn't hear. She couldn't see and she couldn't speak and yet did you know? Of course you do know that this Helen Keller became one of the best educated women in the world. She's in contact with more of public affairs and civic affairs and conditions, all over the world and nine/tenths of the women who have all of their senses.

Isn't that an outstanding thing and all she has to go by is the vibration. And if you speak to her, she puts your fingers up to your lips and she can tell what you're saying by her fingertips, totally by vibration. Think about that woman with a handicap of that kind, all the way through life, getting joy out of life, rendering useful service, making speeches. She's learned after a fashion to talk, doing a great work, where the majority of people would have settled for a tin cap and bunch of lead pencils on a street corner with any one of those afflictions.

While I was on the staff for Franklin D. Roosevelt, I passed at the corner of Pennsylvania Avenue and the street running by the Whitehouse; every day I passed a man sitting there with a tin cup and some pencils. I become acquainted to that man. He had lost the use of his legs and he had the same affliction as Franklin D. Roosevelt exactly and it happened about the same time. And I found out that he had an even a better education than Franklin D. Roosevelt, and I thought very well there he was with a tin cap and pencils trying to eke out a living by begging.

There was a – just a block away, and there was that man with the most important responsible position in the whole world, running a great nation, who also lost the use of his legs but he hadn't lost the use of his brain. He hadn't lost confidence in himself.

These afflictions that come along, sometimes, they'd turn out to be a great blessing. Very often they teach us that we can get along without an eye or without both eyes or without legs or without hands, you can get along without a lot of things. If we have the right mental attitude towards what's left out of us. That's important.

If you would have faith, keep your mind on that which you want and not on that which you do not want. And how do you go about that? How does one go about keeping his mind off of the things he doesn't want?

Look up that word transmute, and see what it means. Look it up in the dictionary, you don't want it to go away, but look it up just for that – because it will be more impressive in your subconscious mind. The way you keep your mind off the things you don't want is to transfer your mind over to things you do want and start talking about them. Start giving thanks for already possessing them.

It will sound perfectly silly to anyone that doesn't know what you're doing, it won't sound silly to you because you know what you're doing, you're talking to your subconscious mind, you're re-educating yourself. You are keeping your mind fixed on things you want and off on the things you don't want and in order to do that, you have to keep talking. You have to keep thinking. You can't talk without thinking, but some people can but most of them can't.

Keep on talking about things you want and if you ever feel blue or discouraged or lacking in courage, I'll tell you a good remedy for it, may I?

Sit down and take a tablet and start numbering, number 1, the things that you want the most in your life, number 2, you want next the most, number 3, the thing you want next most, and when it gets down to the kind of the house you live, describe your lot that you want on. Maybe one of them down the lot of big trees, on top of the hill, or down below the road or above the road, how many rooms you want that house to have, how you want each room furnished and you will have a grand time furnishing those rooms. What is it that you want the most? Well, it will be better than window shopping because you know there's no limit in your mind. In window shopping, you only have two legs and you can only walk so far.

Do a little mental window shopping and believe you me, you'll get your mind over that little issue, you'll get it onto something that's constructive and you'll be educating your subconscious mind to keep on the right side of the street and away from the other side of the railroad tracks.

Next time, what I'm giving you now is not foolish, it's not facetious. It's the real assignment and you'll got real joy out of doing it. Start writing and doing physically. You're writing down the things that you want when anything bothers you.

I don't know why it is, when a person makes up his mind what he wants and becomes determined to get it, that the whole powers of the universe seem to come to his aid to see that he gets it. I don't know why that is, but I tell you one thing; I know that it is and that's enough for me. A lot of things in this world that I can see and one of the advantages I can use it but I don't understand but I don't need to understand them. I know which button to press to get the result I want and I don't need to know what happens between the pressing of that button and the result to see what happens.

I know that if you follow the instructions in this philosophy, I know that you'll be able to take possessions of your mind, you'll be able to get the things out of life that you want and you'll be able to make life pay off on your own terms. I know that. How do I know, do you suppose, that I know that any person can actually make life pay off point by point on his own terms instead of accepting the circumstances? How would I know that?

There is only one way in this world that I could possibly know that and that's by my own experiences. I can tell you as sincerely as I'm standing here on this platform talking to you tonight there isn't a blessed thing in this world that I want that I don't have or can't get easily. Not anything. What an astounding statement that is, if you go back just a few years ago, that's an astonishing statement because it's so broadly in contrast to what I might have said a few years back. Before I learned the secret of getting everything that I want.

Do you know there was a time, when I was carrying around in my own pocket that matches with which I was setting my house of opportunity on fire and I didn't know it. And I finally got rid of those matches. I began to build that house of opportunity and I came to find out that the house resembled the picture of it that I had built in my mind, right down to the finest details. There is no such thing as a blank faith. You must have a definite objective, a purpose, a goal before you can have faith in anything.

Chapter 14 – Faith & How to Pray Effectively

Faith is a mental attitude wherein the mind is cleared of all the fears and doubts and directed toward the attainment of something definite through the inspiration of the Infinite Intelligence. Faith is guidance, it is nothing more. Have you ever thought about that? Faith is guidance, there's nothing more than that? Faith is not going to go out and get you that new house or that Cadillac that you want or that better job or that better business or all those clients that you need if you are a professional, faith is not going to do that. But faith will guide you as to how you can do it and you will find that there is always a part that you must play.

The creator spies the arrangement so that we can produce our food from the soil in the earth. Everything that we eat use or work, comes from the earth, everything. And Infinite Intelligence has very wisely provided a system whereby you can be sure of getting your food out of the soil in the earth. How? By complying with the laws of nature. You go out there and you plant the seed. You plant in soil that you have examined to make sure it has the elements in there that you want in for the plant. You plant it in the right season. You plant it with the right depth in the ground.

All of those things you do by in way of going the extra mile. You do them in advance and then what do you do. You go back the next day and start harvesting, do you?

No, you time it properly, you find out what nature requires in order to produce, to convert or transmute the seed of wheat into a stalk of wheat with 500 or 1,000 grains on it. And you comply with nature's law, that's what you do. And it's the same thing identically in connection with this subject of faith and anything else, you expect the guidance, you do your part. You have to do your part. You will always find that there is a part that you must do in connection with any example of the demonstration of faith.

Faith will do nothing for you if you expect everything to be done for you outside of yourself. It's guidance, that you expect to get the answer that, you'll have it. Well faith probably – now, notice that word probably down there. Why do you think I say faith probably works through the subconscious section of the mind?

I'll tell you why I put it there, because nobody knows definitely whether it does or not. It's a theory and for want of a better theory, I'm using it. It appears to work through the subconscious section of the mind, the subconscious acting as the gateway between the conscious section of the mind and Infinite Intelligence.

My picture, my mental picture of what happens when you pray properly is that you first condition your mind. You know what it is you want and then you transfer over to your subconscious mind a clear picture, that subconscious is the intermediary or the gatekeeper between you and Infinite Intelligence. It's the only one that can turn on the power of Infinite Intelligence for you.

It's the only way you can reach into Infinite Intelligence, in my book of rules. And if that isn't correct, as far as I'm concerned it might as well be correct because that's the way I get it to work.

Now the definite essential step for the development of self-reliance based on faith and if there's anything that people need more than everything else is the self-reliance, belief in yourself.

Here are the steps, I'm not going to go through all of them but I'm going to call your attention to the most important ones.

First of all, about the major purpose and begin it once to attain it, that's the first step in building self-confidence. When you know what you want, and you start in getting it, you have a measure of self-reliance. You're demonstrating a measure of self-reliance because if you didn't believe in yourself, you wouldn't even begin would you.

The very fact that you start even though you're a long way from attaining the thing that you're going after, shows that you have a measure or a degree of self-reliance and the more you pursue that, the stronger that belief will be.

And next associate as many as possible of the 9 basic motives with the object of the definite major purpose. In other words, have yourself inspired by as many as possible, of those 9 basic motives, when you go after anything. You know, you've had this experience that you wanted something very badly and in order to get to something that you wanted very badly, a material something that required extra money that you couldn't lay your hands on, you didn't have it in the bank, you were not earning it, what do you do in a case of that kind?

Borrow? [Laughs]. Well, a lot of people do but there's a lot you can do that is more important part than borrowing. Well, you begin to connive and scheme to work out a plan to earn some more money, don't you?

That's what you do. My little son Blaire when he was about 6 or 7 years old wanted a nice a electrical train that cost about $60. That's more than we thought we can give him at that time because we would have to give the other two children $50 gifts too. And he told told that, "It's alright, you don't have to buy me anything." I said, "Well, that's different. Fine" I just wanted your approval to buy the train. He wrote up the order, Lionel L Trains $50.

And the next day there came a snow, a big snow then he borrowed the shovel from the janitor and he went down the street cleaning outside. He didn't ask if he could do it, he just started cleaning off the sidewalks and all of sudden people would come out and get into a conversation. He would say, "Oh! I thought of a very nice thing. I just cleaned up your sidewalks." He said, "I see you haven't start doing it yet." "I thought it would be nice of you to appreciate it." And people would invariably give him a quarter, half a dollar, sometimes a dollar, one time, a gentleman gave him $5, and before the end of the month, well he had his $50 and $10 more. That he earned himself.

His mother thought that he should not be permitted to do that because it's a disgrace to us to let him go down the street cleaning outside but I said, "Disgrace my eye! They'll find out who we are that we can raise a child like this. How we do it!" [Laughs].

Chapter 15 – Be Success Conscious

Motive, and write out a list of all the advantages of your definite major purpose and call these into your mind many times daily thereby making your mind success conscious.

Did you know that in order to be healthy, you have to be health-conscious? Did you know that? No matter what other big courses you take, if your mental attitude is not health-conscious. If you're not thinking in terms of health, you're not expecting that you're going to be healthy; you're not going to be, no matter what else you do.

And it's the same thing with success, if you accept any kind of a fear complex or an inferiority complex, if you don't expect success of yourself and develop a success expectation or consciousness, you're not going to be a success. You just have to do that.

If your major purpose is to achieve some material thing or money, see yourself already in possession of it. When you call it into your consciousness, this is a vital importance because there again, is coming into play your power of faith. And if your faith isn't great enough so that you see the thing already in your possession even before you start to get it done then you're not making use of applied faith.

And associate with people who are in symphony with you and your major purpose and lead them to encourage you in every way possible. This has reference only to close friends or members of your mastermind alliance. Don't disclose your aims and purposes to people who are not absolutely dependable, loyal and close to you, especially loyal.

You'll be surprised sometimes people to whom you disclose your ideas, if they're good ideas, they go around the corner and beat you to the draw and will go out there using your ideas before you do or they're saying something to discourage you. **And let not a single day**

pass without making at least one definite move towards the attainment of your definite major purpose. Faith is a positive mental attitude in action and your mental attitude is reflected in every word you speak and it speaks louder than your words. Your mental attitude is the sum total of your thoughts at a given time.

A positive mental attitude has its roots in the spiritual wealth of one's soul. How true that is and what a wonderful statement that is. **A positive mental attitude has its roots in the spiritual wealth of one's soul**. Mental attitude is the medium by which adversities may be transmuted into benefits and so the list goes.

Now, you find some of those and as you see more than those, print them out and on a card or in some form where you can put them up where you can see them each day. Make them your own, surround yourself with suggestions. Everywhere you look, you'll see something that suggests the positive mental attitude.

When you go into the office of a successful person or into the home of a successful person, if you can find his den or the place where he withdraws unto himself, you will find that often times, he has himself surrounded with pictures of those whom he considers great. Often times, they will have mottos on the walls, I've seen hundreds of them. I walked into Ed Barnes office one time and I found out that he had over 500 mottos done up in beautiful cards, hand-lettered, every one of them and must have cost him a small fortune.

I walked into my friends Jennings Randolph's' Office when he was in Congress and walked in and I found he had all in the walls of his Congressional Office covered with the pictures of people whom he considered great. He did that to live in the environment of the great and in the environment of things that kept his mind positive.

Start off in where you are, in your home, in your business, in your office, wherever you stay the most, maybe it's in your bedroom where you sleep every night. Start in there to put up something that will give you a positive thought just before you go to bed and that reminds you every time you go in there.

Afterword

I hope you have been inspired by this book; if so please consider sending a gift copy to a friend. Continue your training and build your library of success – institutional education can prepare you for a job and a career but training for personal success is left up to you. Be sure to get the next volume in the series from Amazon! It is available at:

http://www.amazon.com/dp/B009BONVB6

You may now also get the Complete Rare Volume collection in Kindle or paperback editions at:

http://www.amazon.com/dp/B00C7SL1I8

May you achieve all your goals in record time!

~ Patrick Doucette

Printed in Great Britain
by Amazon.co.uk, Ltd.,
Marston Gate.